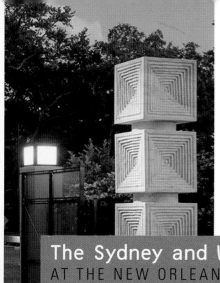

MIRANDA LASH

D1519833

The Sydney and Walda Besthoff Sculpture Garden
AT THE NEW ORLEANS MUSEUM OF ART
ART SPACES

In 2003, the New Orleans Museum of Art (NOMA) inaugurated the Sydney and Walda Besthoff Sculpture Garden. The nearly five-acre Garden, adjacent to the Museum in City Park, opened with fifty works of art by modern and contemporary artists of international renown, including Henry Moore, Barbara Hepworth, George Segal, and Louise Bourgeois. Its sculptures are installed in an expansive natural setting amongst meandering footpaths, reflecting lagoons, live oaks, mature pines, and magnolias. The first years of the Garden's existence witnessed a spectrum of events, including the struggle and recovery following Hurricane Katrina. Today the Garden boasts sixty-three works of art (a number which continues to grow), and is widely recognized as one of the foremost sculpture gardens in the United States. Its design earned awards from the American Society of Landscape Architects in 2006 and the American Institute of Architects in 2007.

← Entrance to the Sydney and Walda Besthoff Sculpture Garden

↑ Aerial view of the Garden

Sydney and Walda Besthoff

Known as connoisseurs of modern and contemporary sculpture, Sydney and Walda Besthoff founded their Garden for the aim of allowing the public to enjoy art in a contemplative and idyllic Louisiana environment. Both lifelong New Orleanians, for many decades the Besthoffs have been (and continue to be) important business and cultural leaders in New Orleans. Sydney Besthoff served as chairman and CEO of the family-owned retail drugstore chain K & B (Katz and Besthoff) Incorporated, which his grandfather founded in 1905. After an extensive period of expansion under Sydney Besthoff's direction, K & B was sold to the Rite Aid Corporation in 1997. Sydney Besthoff has served on the boards of numerous business and arts organizations and was a founder of the Contemporary Arts Center (CAC) of New Orleans. Walda Besthoff maintains an enduring commitment to the performing arts as a performer, staffer, and patron. She has served on numerous boards, including at the CAC and NOMA.

The Besthoffs' interest in collecting sculpture began in 1973. That year they acquired an office building at Lee Circle in New Orleans to serve as the corporate headquarters for K & B Incorporated. The Chicago architectural firm Skidmore, Owings & Merrill had designed the building in 1961 for John Hancock Insurance. For the large plaza surrounding the building, the architects commissioned an eighteen-foot-high granite fountain by Isamu Noguchi, *The Mississippi*, 1961–62. Water is meant to spill from the fountain's crescent-shaped top, alluding to the Mississippi River's role in shaping New Orleans into the Crescent City. Unfortunately, when the Besthoffs purchased the building, Noguchi's water feature was not functioning. Sydney Besthoff's subsequent investigation into the fountain's repair sparked his enduring interest in the mechanics of sculpture.

With the Noguchi restored, the Besthoffs commissioned their first work of art, George Rickey's *Four Open Rectangles Excentric, Square Section,* 1978, after consulting E. John Bullard, then the new director of NOMA. The museum owned a small example of Rickey's work, and Rickey (who taught at Newcomb College at Tulane

← Sydney and Walda Besthoff, 2010

Sculptures on the K & B Plaza:

→ Isamu Noguchi,
   The Mississippi, 1961–62

↠ George Rickey, *Four Open
   Rectangles Excentric,
   Square Section*, 1978.
   Art © Estate of George Rickey/
   Licensed by VAGA, New York, NY

University from 1955 to 1962) sent Sydney Besthoff 8mm films of his sculptures in motion. Interested in these kinetic features, Sydney purchased a second work by Rickey, *Four Lines Oblique,* 1973–77, which is now in his namesake Garden. In 1977, the Besthoffs established the Sydney and Walda Besthoff Foundation (also known as the Virlane Foundation, after their three daughters Virgina, Jane, and Valerie). Thereafter, the growth of their modern and contemporary collection accelerated. They installed numerous large-scale works on the building's plaza and displayed smaller sculptures and paintings throughout their corporate headquarters.

Among the Besthoffs' earliest sculpture acquisitions were works by some of the most important sculptors of the twentieth century, including Henry Moore, Barbara Hepworth, and Jacques Lipchitz. The Besthoffs traveled extensively in Europe and encountered work by British, Italian, and, of particular interest, French artists. As Walda Besthoff explains, "The New Orleans Museum of Art has a fantastic collection of nineteenth-century French paintings, and we wanted the continuity of the French feel. We are the only European city in America."[1]

↑ Jesús Moroles, *Las Mesas Bench,* 1989, and Henry Moore, *Reclining Mother and Child,* 1975

As their preferences evolved, the Besthoffs also sought the work of younger artists such as Saint Clair Cemin, Rona Pondick, and Jean-Michel Othoniel. "When we first started collecting," Walda Besthoff recalls, "we were not sure of ourselves, so we bought names. We bought things we thought were fairly classic. As time went on we became more aware of who was producing what and we let our own taste govern what we were buying."[2] Sydney Besthoff agrees, "We zero in on particular artists, rather than use a scattershot approach."[3]

After several decades of collecting, K & B Headquarters boasted a broad and impressive selection of twentieth-century art, which remains open for public viewing. In addition to sculpture, the Besthoffs became avid collectors of American photorealist painting, acquiring important works by Richard Estes, Ralph Goings, and Robert Cottingham.

Genesis of the Garden

In 1992, discussions began among Sydney and Walda Besthoff, NOMA, and the City Park Improvement Association about the future of the Besthoff Foundation collection. These conversations led to the creation of a sculpture garden to permanently display the large-scale works of the Besthoff collection. The Besthoff Foundation agreed to donate the sculptures to the Museum and also a generous percentage of the construction funds needed

to build the Garden. City Park provided a site adjacent to the Museum at the cost of one dollar per year for one hundred years. NOMA committed to raise the funds necessary to construct the Garden and maintain it in perpetuity. The Museum also agreed to augment the Garden with suitable works from its permanent collection.

Design of the Garden

The design of the Garden was entrusted to project architect Lee Ledbetter of Lee Ledbetter Architects, New Orleans, and landscape architect Brian Sawyer of Sawyer/Berson, New York. Ledbetter and Sawyer were familiar with each other's work, having both been previously employed in the offices of Robert A. M. Stern Architects in New York.

In planning the design of the Garden, it was apparent that the original, extraordinary qualities of the City Park landscape should be preserved as much as possible. Ledbetter and Sawyer therefore faced the unique challenge of adapting their design to a pre-existing lagoon and the mature growth of pine trees and live oaks, some

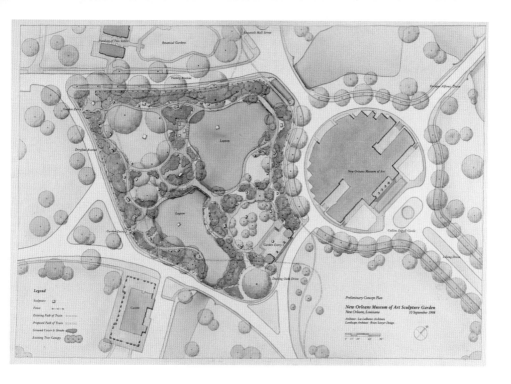

Pavilion of Two Sisters

Botanical Gardens

Roosevelt Mall Street

Victory Avenue

Portland Alfonso Street

Lagoon

Lelong Entry

Dreyfous Avenue

New Orleans Museum of Art

Lagoon

Garden Entry

Collins Diboll Circle

Garden Entry

Lelong Drive

Dueling Oaks Drive

Legend

Sculpture

Fence

Existing Path of Train

Proposed Path of Train

Ground Cover & Shrubs

Existing Tree Canopy

Casino

Preliminary Concept Plan

New Orleans Museum of Art Sculpture Garden
New Orleans, Louisiana   *10 September 1998*

Architect · Lee Ledbetter Architects
Landscape Architect · Brian Sawyer Design

Previous page:
Panoramic view of the
Pine Grove

↑ Pavilion at the main entrance
to the Garden

↗ Henry Moore, *Reclining
Mother and Child,* 1975

over two hundred years old. Ledbetter and Sawyer considered the "intrinsic beauty" of the site to be its most important asset, and their primary goal was to enhance its character.[4] The molding of the Garden's design around its existing vegetation and bodies of water distinguishes it from gardens that are more traditionally based on a superimposed grid pattern. Sydney Besthoff explains: "The architectural concept has no straight lines, everything is curved. It's a real English countryside garden, in the style of Capability Brown. We specifically wanted to get away from the Italian Renaissance and the French formal look, which most sculpture gardens adopt."[5]

Ledbetter and Sawyer's assessment of the land led them to plan the site around an implied axis, with the "front" facing Dreyfous Meadow and the "back" pointing towards the New Orleans Botanical Garden. A pair

of square, cast stone and bronze pavilions flanking the Garden's main entrance (one housing a visitor's desk and another housing restrooms), further establishes this axis. The pavilions' clean, geometric design complements the 1990 wings of the Museum facing the Garden. Their orientation to the Meadow echoes the Museum's orientation to Lelong Avenue. The main entrance is further distinguished by a stepped limestone plaza, which showcases Henry Moore's *Reclining Mother and Child*, 1975, one of the Garden's masterpieces. Secondary entrances at the Garden's "wings" face City Park's Casino (its entrance marked by Gaston Lachaise's *Heroic Man*, 1928–35), and the Botanical Garden (distinguished by Minoru Niizuma's *Castle of the Eye, II*, 1973). The existing landscape also led the architects to conceive of the Garden in zones: the Pine Grove at the entrance, the

↖ Side entrance with Gaston Lachaise, *Heroic Man*, 1928–35

↑ Back entrance with Minoru Niizuma, *Castle of the Eye, II*, 1973

↑ Ossip Zadkine, *La Poetesse*, 1953 with Yaacov Agam, *Open Space*, 1970

bisected Lagoon in the center, and the Oak Grove at the back. These zones were then further adapted to allow visitors multiple possible routes around the Garden. Pedestrian bridges cross the lagoon in three different locations, and the meandering pathways make small loops. The overall design encourages a sense of exploration and discovery, as the sculptures are revealed to the visitors over the course of their walk.

The Garden's layout also accommodates the sculptures' various sizes. Monumental works such as Claes Oldenburg and Coosje Van Bruggen's *Corridor Pin, Blue*, 1999, and Louise Bourgeois's *Spider*, 1996, are situated in the open space of the Oak Grove. Meanwhile smaller works, such as William Zorach's *Future Generations*, 1942–47, and Leonard Baskin's *Ruth and Naomi*, 1979, are framed against niches of shrubbery in the Sculpture

Theater. The long vistas afforded by the large Lagoon provide ideal viewing for the towering structures of Arman's *Pablo Casals's Obelisk*, 1983, and Kenneth Snelson's *Virlane Tower*, 1981. The Cascade Pool, located in the Garden's center, is partitioned off from the Lagoon by a stepping-stone path, creating an intimate viewing area for Robert Graham's *Source Figure*, 1991. Scott Burton's *Settee* and *Pair of Right Angle Chairs*, both 1983,

bookend the Cascade Pool, providing a functional role as seats for visitors to contemplate the Lagoon. The stepping-stone path at the Pool is deliberately reminiscent of the Ryōan-ji Temple Garden in Kyoto. As Sawyer explained, "Lee and I looked at a lot of Japanese gardens, we thought that their essence and their simplicity were appropriate to consider when creating a backdrop for sculpture."[6]

↑ Robert Indiana, *LOVE Red Blue*, 1966–97 and Louise Bourgeois, *Spider*, 1996.
Art © Estate of Louise Bourgeois Trust/Licensed by VAGA, New York, NY

This page:

→ Sculpture Theater with George Segal, *Three Figures and Four Benches*, 1979 and William Zorach, *Future Generations*, 1942–47, and Leonard Baskin, *Ruth and Naomi*, 1979.

↓ Lagoon with Fritz Bultman, *Barrier (Big Bird)*, 1967–70

Opposite page:

→ Lagoon with Arman, *Pablo Casals's Obelisk*, 1983, and Jesús Moroles, *Las Mesas Benches*, 1989

↓ Exedra with Stephen de Staebler, *Standing Man with Outstretched Arm*, 1987

↠ Kenneth Snelson, *Virlane Tower*, 1981

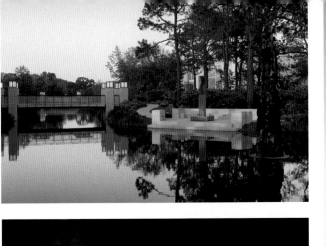

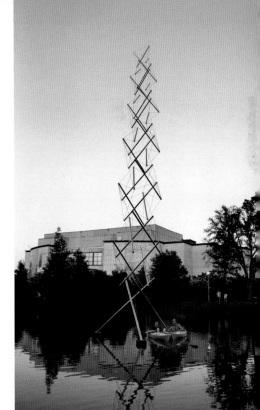

↑ Cascade Pool with Scott Burton's *Pair of Right Angle Chairs* and *Settee*, 1983, and Robert Graham's *Source Figure*, 1991

→ Construction of a bridge crossing the Lagoon

↓ Construction of the main entrance Pavilions

⇢ Dredging of the Lagoon to install Arman, *Pablo Casals's Obelisk*, 1983

Construction of the Garden

Once the Garden design was agreed upon, the groundbreaking occurred on June 29, 2001. Construction took approximately two and a half years. The Lagoon was temporarily drained to install the sculptures by Arman and Snelson and to create a path for hauling construction material. A significant amount of the Garden's expense was allocated to ensuring the trees' survival through the construction process and promoting their long-term health.[7] Throughout the construction process arborists were on site to provide root therapy, feeding, mulching, and shaping. While some storm-damaged and disease-infested trees were removed, replacements came in, resulting in a net gain of trees.

With the landscaping of the Garden complete, the individual sculptures were installed. This process often required a foundation to be dug into the soil, a concrete platform laid, a base designed and built, and the sculpture itself wrapped and lifted by crane into place. Sydney Besthoff recalls, "We sited each sculpture where we thought it was best—a four-way mutual

→ Craning of Fernando
   Botero, *Mother and Child,*
   1988, over the Garden wall

↠ Botero's *Mother and Child*
   in flight

discussion—myself, the museum director, the architect, and the landscape architect."[8] While the Garden was not laid out with a specific chronology in mind, the majority of the artists affiliated with the late nineteenth and early twentieth century were placed in the Pine Grove. More contemporary works gravitated towards the Oak Grove. "What is great about the dual garden model," Walda Besthoff explains, "is that you cannot help but see how sculpture evolved in the twentieth and twenty-first centuries."[9]

On November 23, 2003, the Sydney and Walda Besthoff Sculpture Garden opened with fifty sculptures—forty-one donated by the Besthoff Foundation, combined with nine works from the Museum's permanent collection.

← Sydney Besthoff approves *Mother and Child*'s final placement

↑ Oak Grove in 2003

≪≪The aftermath of Hurricane Katrina: Snelson's *Virlane Tower*

≪ Water lines on Scott Burton's *Settee*

← Oregon National Guardsmen clear fallen trees and debris in 2005

Hurricane Katrina and the Flooding of New Orleans

In its first years the Garden enjoyed an inspiring degree of enthusiasm from its visitors and glowing reviews in local and national press. Its tranquility was relatively short-lived however. On August 29, 2005, Hurricane Katrina struck eastern Louisiana. While the storm's direct damage to New Orleans was not severe, the ensuing failure of fifty-three levee walls submerged eighty-percent of the city. The resulting financial damage (estimated between $125 billion and $250 billion) and psychological pain caused by Hurricane Katrina and the flooding of New Orleans is impossible to quantify. NOMA was forced to layoff eighty-five percent of its staff. Although the Museum building did not flood, and the artworks inside were unharmed, the same was not true of the Garden, whose *Virlane Tower* by Snelson was destroyed (the artist later rebuilt the work).

Together the Museum and the Garden sustained approximately $6 million in damage.[10] In the Garden forty trees blew down during the storm, and thirty percent

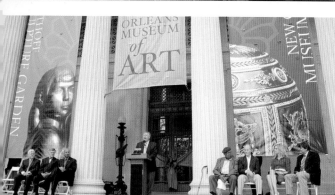

This page:
← Garden manager Pamela Buckman and volunteer David Averbuck at the Garden's reopening in 2010

← An air spade is used to remove and aerate the compromised soil

Opposite page:
← John Ward cleans Robert Indiana, *LOVE Red Blue, 1966–97*

← NOMA reopens after Hurricane Katrina in 2006. Director E. John Bullard at podium with Mayor Ray Nagin seated to his immediate right.

← Volunteers plant irises

of the ground cover and bushes were decimated. The flooding rendered the Garden's irrigation and electrical systems inoperable. The Oak Grove was submerged under several feet of toxic water for over two weeks. While museum professionals flew in from all over the country to preserve the permanent collection at NOMA, the Garden was fortunate to have immediate assistance from the National Guard, who assisted in cutting down damaged trees and clearing debris. Museum staff, contractors, and volunteers sprang into action cleaning the sculptures and replanting.

→ Auguste Rodin, *Monumental Head of Jean d'Aire* (from *The Burghers of Calais*), c. 1884–86; enlarged 1909–10

After being closed for only four and a half months, the Sculpture Garden reopened on December 10, 2005, providing a space of meditation for the citizens of New Orleans as they began the tremendous task of rebuilding their city. NOMA reopened on March 3, 2006, with hundreds of visitors arriving on the first day. Although the Museum was initially only able to open its doors three days a week, its return was a symbolic touchstone for the city. As director E. John Bullard explained, "As soon as the storm and immediate crisis passed and the extent of the devastation was revealed, something else was crucially apparent: art and culture are not luxuries, but necessities—sources of solace, comfort, perspective, inspiration, and rejuvenation."[11]

Following the storm, nineteen historic live oaks in the Garden were in danger as the flooding and salt intrusion compacted the soil and deprived their roots of oxygen.[12] This threat was compounded by four months of drought following the storm and the lack of a functioning irrigation system. However, neither the Federal Emergency Management Agency (FEMA), nor the museum's insurance provided funds for the restoration of plants. In 2007 the Getty Foundation awarded a much-needed grant for the preservation and replacement of the oaks and shrubs. The process of aerating the soil, adding drainage, and carefully restoring the trees began on October 1, 2007, during which time the Oak Grove was temporarily closed. By the spring of 2009, the oaks were on the path to recovery.

After several years of assessment and negotiations, FEMA agreed to repair the damage caused to the infrastructure of the Garden due to flooding. The Garden closed to the public in August 2009 for these repairs to take place. Contractors were hired to reconstruct the electrical, lighting, and irrigation systems, mend the walkways, and reinforce the Lagoon banks. The final reopening of the Garden on March 20, 2010, was a joyous occasion, augmented by the unveiling of a donation from the Iris and B. Gerald Cantor Foundation: the *Monumental Head of Jean d'Aire*, c. 1884–86, from *The Burghers of Calais* by Auguste Rodin. The selfless heroism of Jean d'Aire, a burgher who offered to sacrifice himself for his city, was a fitting tribute to hundreds of volunteers and donors who made the reopening of the Garden possible.

Present Day

Today the vibrantly restored Sydney and Walda Besthoff Sculpture Garden is a jewel in the city of New Orleans, complete with a roster of public programming and special events. On scheduled days visitors to the Garden can take classes in yoga, pilates, and tai chi; watch outdoor films; ride gondolas through the Lagoon; and listen to

↓ Afternoon in the Pine Grove

≪ Oak Grove with Elisabeth Frink's *Riace Warriors I, II, III, IV*, 1983–88

≪ Azaleas frame Ida Kohlmeyer, *Rebus 3D-89-3*, 1989

← Yoga in the Garden

<<< Gondola on the Lagoon

← Louisiana irises

← Augustus Saint-Gaudens,
   Diana, 1886; cast 1985

live music. Each year the Garden hosts an Iris Viewing Festival in April, a Fabergé Egg Hunt around Easter, and the evening soiree "Love in the Garden" in September.

Thanks to the ongoing generosity of Sydney and Walda Besthoff, the artwork in the Garden continues to expand, including the recent addition of a mirror piece, *Untitled*, 1997, by Anish Kapoor to the Oak Grove, and the gilt huntress *Diana* by Augustus Saint-Gaudens (modeled 1886; cast 1985) to the Pine Grove. These two sculptures—one exemplifying the height of idealized classicism in human figuration, and another demonstrating the latest strides in contemporary abstraction—demonstrate the range of the Besthoffs' interests. In addition to seeking quality in both modern and contemporary art, their commitment to sharing their interests with the broader public is truly admirable. The Garden remains an evolving testament to their taste and philanthropy.

→ Pierre-Auguste Renoir, *Venus Victorious*, 1914, and Antoine Bourdelle, *Hercules the Archer*, 1909 (cast 1947)

Highlights of the Garden

While the sixty-three sculptures on view in the Sydney and Walda Besthoff Sculpture Garden represent a wide diversity of artistic styles, many of the works cluster around themes. The Besthoffs' collecting gravitates toward certain nationalities, including works by French, British, Italian, Japanese, Israeli, and American artists. Specific movements and subjects are also recurrent, among them the human figuration, geometric abstraction, Surrealism, and Pop art. The Besthoffs are not rigidly exclusive in their collecting, and there are a number of works that do not fit neatly into any category. The following is meant as a general guide for the visitor to seven themes in the Garden:

French Sculpture at the Turn of the Twentieth Century

The foundational artist in this group is Auguste Rodin, whose expressive departure from neoclassicism provided the model and the foil against which his French

→ Aristide Maillol, *Venus Without Arms*, 1922

⇢ Barbara Hepworth, *River Form*, 1965

counterparts worked. One can perceive the influence of Rodin in the intensely articulated musculature of Antoine Bourdelle's *Hercules the Archer*, 1909 (cast 1947). A student, assistant, and friend to Rodin, Bourdelle nonetheless sought his particular stamp on the human figure, in this case by adhering to a strong sense of geometry. As Hercules enacts the sixth of his labors, shooting the Stymphalian birds, the work is governed by the semi-circle of his bow and the dynamic angles of his limbs and supporting rocks. The more classically inspired works, *Venus Without Arms*, 1922, by Aristide Maillol and *Venus Victorious*, 1914, by Pierre-Auguste Renoir (executed with the assistance of Richard Guino), offer a comparatively restrained approach to the human figure. The two idealized Venuses demonstrate the artists' obsession with line, contour, and volume. Renoir's *Venus* is the oldest sculpture in the Garden (based on the date of its casting).

British Abstraction

In the sculpture of British artists Henry Moore and Barbara Hepworth an entirely different approach to

abstraction becomes apparent, one that emphasizes a dialogue between positive and negative space, and focuses on curvilinear forms over geometric angularity. Moore and Hepworth were friends and classmates. They met in 1919, and both studied at Leeds School of Art and later at the Royal College of Art in London. While Hepworth became known in the early twentieth century for sculpting in an almost entirely abstract manner, Moore became famous for his biomorphic figures. The holes and concavities in Hepworth's *River Form*, 1965, evoke the movement of water through sedimentary stones. In his *Reclining Mother and Child*, Moore revisits one of his preferred subjects: maternity. The design for this work was likely influenced by his time sketching pre-Columbian art in the British Museum as a young artist. Coming from a younger generation, Lynn Chadwick was inspired by Moore's use of figural abstraction. However, his *Sitting Figures (2)*, 1979–80, with ominously blank square faces, convey a sharpness and planarity in contrast to Moore.

Surrealism

Famous for its tendency towards the fantastical and extreme, New Orleans seems an appropriate home for works with a Surrealist tendency. René Magritte's *The Labors of Alexander,* 1967, creates a riddle through the juxtaposition of objects, as is typical of his work. The root of a tree stump extends over an ax, leading the viewer to question which object has triumphed in this situation: the ax or tree? Originally based on a painting with the same nonsensical title, *The Labors of Alexander* was posthumously cast in bronze. Magritte was directly associated with the Surrealists, beginning in Paris during the 1920s. Meanwhile Louise Bourgeois, whose works also carry a Surrealist element, worked for forty years in obscurity. Her imposing *Spider* is one of a series of arachnids associated with the artist's mother. Descending from a family of weavers, Bourgeois explains, "My best friend was my mother and she was…dainty, subtle, indispensable, neat, and as useful as a spider."[13]

The influence of Surrealism continues to surface in contemporary art as in Rona Pondick's *Monkeys,*

← Lynn Chadwick, *Sitting Figures (2)*, 1979–80

<< Louise Bourgeois, *Spider*,
1996.

Art © Louise Bourgeois Trust/
Licensed by VAGA, New York, NY

← René Magritte, *The Labors
of Alexander*, 1967

1998–2001. Pondick explores the theme of hybridity by melding casts of her own hands and face to a gleaming tangle of monkeys. Though often associated with the controversies surrounding human evolution and genetic manipulation, Pondick also relates her *Monkeys* to Franz Kafka's 1915 novella *The Metamorphosis*.

Italian Art after World War II

The Italian artists in the Garden demonstrate the diversity of styles to emerge from Italy after World War II. In 1947, Pietro Consagra, inspired by artists such as Constantin Brancusi and Pablo Picasso, helped found the group Forma I, which emphasized both formalism and Marxism. Consagra's *Conversation with the Moon*, 1960, reflects his interest in working in layers of low relief, emphasizing the frontality of the sculpture. Consagra was associated with the Continuità group, founded in 1961 as an outgrowth of Forma I. Arnaldo Pomodoro, also a member of Continuità, similarly promoted the importance of abstraction. His piece *A Battle: For the Resistance Fighters*, 1971, which depicts an overturned obelisk crushing its base, was commissioned by the city of Modena as a memorial to the resistance fighters of World War II.

Out of the 1960s also came the Arte Povera movement, which advocated for a "poor" art of basic materials—twigs, stone, glass, and fabric, and a more conceptual and experimental approach to art making. Luciano Fabro's *The Day Weighs on My Night, V,* 2000, highlights both the raw and carved quality of marble stone. Meanwhile, abstaining from any specific movement was Giacomo Manzù, a devoutly Catholic artist. His streamlined and impassive *Large Seated Cardinal*, 1983, is a typical example of his focus on religious themes and personages.

← Rona Pondick, *Monkeys*, 1998–2001

← Arnaldo Pomodoro, *A Battle: For the Resistance Fighters*, 1971

← Luciano Fabro, *The Day Weighs on My Night, V*, 2000

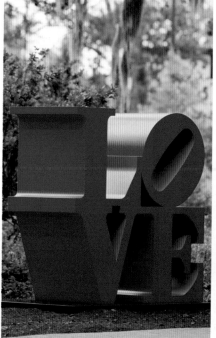

→ Giacomo Manzù, *Large Seated Cardinal,* 1983

↠ Robert Indiana, *LOVE, Red Blue,* 1966–97

↠↠ Claes Oldenburg and Coosje van Bruggen, *Corridor Pin, Blue,* 1999, and Joel Shapiro, *Untitled,* 1991

Pop Art

The Pop artists of the 1950s and 1960s, so called for their interest in popular culture, unsurprisingly produced some of the most approachable works in the Garden. Rebelling against the highly individualized approach of the Abstract Expressionists who preceded them, Pop artists sought to create work that was accessible to everyone, often using the language of advertising, comic books, and everyday household objects. Robert Indiana's *LOVE, Red Blue*, 1966–97, is adored by visitors for its bright colors and clear proclamation of the endearing subject of "love." Pop art also deals, however, with the theoretical implications surrounding commercialization. *LOVE, Red Blue* demonstrates how even a sacred and intangible concept such as love can be made into a commodity. Oldenburg and van Bruggen's *Corridor Pin, Blue* is a typical example of the husband-and-wife team's practice of enlarging mundane objects to a colossal scale. The humble safety pin, normally a cheap, mass-produced item, is elevated to a monumental, aesthetically dynamic status. Pop artist George Segal approached contemporary

culture through a different angle, instead focusing on people moving through public spaces such as cafés, bus stations, and benches, such as in *Three Figures and Four Benches*, 1979. His life-size casts capture individuals in moments of introspective contemplation.

Geometric Abstraction

The Besthoffs' interest in abstraction began through the work of George Rickey, an artist initially inspired by the mobiles of Alexander Calder. His *Four Lines Oblique*, made of four swiveling spears, finds its companion in lightness and dynamism in Snelson's *Virlane Tower*. A student of the engineer and architect Buckminster Fuller, Snelson's constructions operate on the principle of "tensegrity" or tension and integrity between the stainless steel tubes and cables.

The late twentieth-century work of geometric abstraction in the Garden, while not strictly minimalist, often reflects a dialogue with the discourse of minimalism in the cleanness of its design. The blocky geometric forms of Joel Shapiro depart from minimalism in their connection to the human figure. Shapiro's *Untitled*, 1991, for example, suggests a torso and limbs. Scott Burton similarly adheres to a minimalist sensibility, yet departs from pure formalism by making works that are also functional furniture, such as his *Settee* and *Pair of Right Angle Chairs*, 1983.

← George Segal, *Three Figures and Four Benches*, 1979.
Art © The George and Helen Segal Foundation/Licensed by VAGA, New York, NY

← George Rickey, *Four Lines Oblique*, 1973–77 and Kenneth Snelson, *Virlane Tower*, 1981.
Art © Estate of George Rickey/ Licensed by VAGA, New York, NY

↑ Allan McCollum, *Perfect Vehicles*, 1988

→ Alison Saar, *Travelin' Light*, 1999 and Saint Clair Cemin, *Acme*, 1990

Art at the Turn of Twenty-first Century

Contemporary art from the last twenty-five years has been marked by the dispersion of ideas over codified movements. Its most prevalent concerns often relate to globalization, subjectivity, audience participation, social justice, and identity politics. In *Perfect Vehicles*, 1988, Allan McCollum's jars can be exhibited ad infinitum, each displaying a slightly different color. Drawing on the use of repetition in Pop art, McCollum's vehicles explore the possibility of individuality in the context of mass production. In *Travelin' Light*, 1999, Alison Saar opens a dialogue into the history of racial struggle in the United States. Though her suspended figure relates to the lynching of African Americans, the work also speaks to human rights abuses worldwide. Saar's stoic man doubles as a bell, which is rung by pulling a chain in his back. French artist Jean-Michel Othoniel delves into the complex history of New Orleans in his *Tree of Necklaces*, 2002. His colorful Venetian glass beads hanging in the Oak Grove recall the leftover Mardi Gras beads that remain in New Orleans' trees year-round. At five feet tall, however, the size of the necklaces deliberately refers to the size of a human, which, like *Travelin' Light*, connects to the hangings of African Americans during the time of racial segregation.

Leandro Erlich's *Window and Ladder—Too Late for Help*, 2008, was previously installed in the Lower Ninth Ward, an area of New Orleans devastated by the failure of the levees in 2005. In that context, the piece was seemingly a critique of the disaster and its human toll. Its relocation to the Garden opens new possibilities of interpretation.

→ Jean-Michel Othoniel, *Tree of Necklaces*, 2002, and Louise Bourgeois, *Spider*.

⇥ Leandro Erlich, *Window and Ladder—Too Late for Help*, 2008

New Orleans Museum of Art

The New Orleans Museum of Art, situated in City Park, is the city's oldest fine arts institution. In 1910, Isaac Delgado, a sugar cane plantation owner, provided the funds to build an art museum, which he envisioned as a "temple of art for rich and poor alike." The result was a 25,000-square-foot, classically inspired Beaux Arts building, originally named the Isaac Delgado Museum of Art. Although the museum opened in 1911 without owning a single work of art, today it boasts a magnificent permanent collection of nearly 40,000 objects. Having expanded its building in 1972 and 1993, NOMA is recognized as one of the foremost museums of the American South.

The collection is noted for its strengths in European and American painting, photography, decorative arts, African art, Japanese art, art of the Americas, and Louisiana art. Reflecting its rich colonial heritage, NOMA holds an expansive survey of French art, including masterpieces by Claude Lorrain, Elisabeth Vigée-Lebrun, Jean-Leon Gérôme, Edgar Degas, Édouard Vuillard, and George Braque, among others.

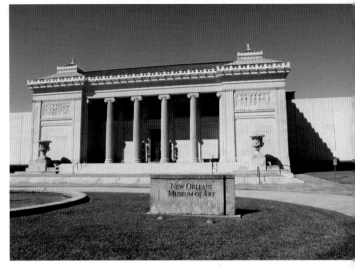

↑ New Orleans Museum of Art

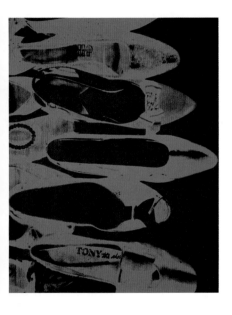

While best known for their contributions to their namesake Garden, Sydney and Walda Besthoff have also provided extraordinary gifts to the collection within the Museum's walls. Their donations often reflect their interests in sculpture, some of the most notable examples being the Italian Futurist Umberto Boccioni's *Unique Forms of Continuity in Space*, 1913; cast 1972, and French artist Yves Klein's *Venus Bleue*, 1962; cast 1982. In addition to sculpture, the Besthoffs have donated significant paintings, including Pop artist James Rosenquist's *Pop Eye, Speed of Light*, 2001, and Andy Warhol's *Diamond Dust Shoes*, 1980–81.

⋘ The Great Hall at the New Orleans Museum of Art

⋘ Umberto Boccioni, *Unique Forms of Continuity in Space*, 1913; cast 1972

← Andy Warhol, *Diamond Dust Shoes*, 1980–81.
© 2011 The Andy Warhol Foundation for the Visual Arts / Artists Rights Society (ARS) New York

→ James Rosenquist, *Pop Eye-
Speed of Light,* 2001.

Art © James Rosenquist/Licensed
by VAGA, New York, NY

Notes

1. Sydney and Walda Besthoff, interview by Miranda Lash in *Great Collectors Great Donors at the New Orleans Museum of Art*, DVD, directed by Kevin McCaffrey and John d'Addario (New Orleans: New Orleans Museum of Art, 2010).

2. William Fagaly, " An Interview with Sydney and Walda Besthoff," *Arts Quarterly: New Orleans Museum of Art* 22, no. 3 (2000): 19–22.

3. Robert Preece, "Collecting New Orleans-Style: A Conversation with Sydney Besthoff," *Sculpture* 23, no. 8 (2004): 30.

4. William Fagaly, "An Interview with Architect Lee Ledbetter and Landscape Architect Brian Sawyer," *Arts Quarterly: New Orleans Museum of Art* 22, no. 2 (2000): 19–22.

5. Preece, "Collecting New Orleans-Style," 29.

6. Fagaly, "Interview with Architect," 22.

7. Lake Douglas, "The Landscape Architecture of the Sydney and Walda Besthoff Sculpture Garden," *Arts Quarterly: New Orleans Museum of Art* 26, no. 1 (2004): 14–15.

8. Preece, "Collecting New Orleans-Style," 29.

9. Sydney and Walda Besthoff, interview in *Great Collectors Great Donors*.

10. New Orleans Museum of Art, "NOMA Survives Katrina," *Arts Quarterly: New Orleans Museum of Art* 28, no. 1 (2006): 1–2.

11. Press release, "The Big Easy in The Big Apple: Two Centuries of Art in Louisiana From the Battle of New Orleans to Katrina," loan exhibition from the New Orleans Museum of Art to AXA Gallery, March 10– May 20, 2006.

12. Meg Adams, "Oak Tree Restoration at NOMA's Sydney and Walda Besthoff Sculpture Garden," *Arts Quarterly: New Orleans Museum of Art* 30, no. 2 (2008): 18–19.

13. Elaine Reichek, "Spider's Stratagem," *Art in America* 96, no. 8 (2008): 119.

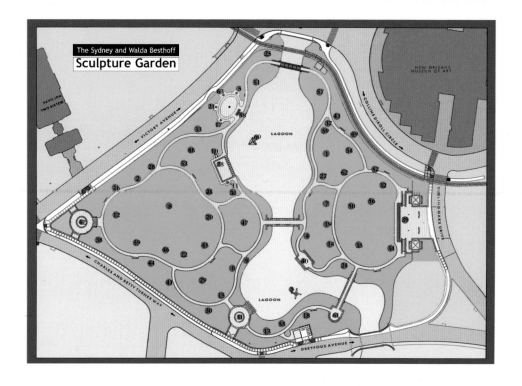

The Sydney and Walda Besthoff
Sculpture Garden

**Works in the Sydney and
Walda Besthoff Sculpture
Garden at the New Orleans
Museum of Art**

*Unless otherwise indicated,
works listed are gifts from the
Sydney and Walda Besthoff
Foundation*

1. Yaacov Agam
   Israeli, born 1928
   Open Space, 1970
   Stainless steel
   108 x 96 x 96 in.
   1998.127

2. Siah Armajani
   American, born in Iran, 1939
   Elements #29, 1991
   Painted steel
   114 x 80 x 79 ½ in.
   1998.128

3. Arman (Armand Pierre
   Fernandez)
   French, 1928–2005
   Pablo Casals's Obelisk, 1983
   Bronze
   240 x 84 x 60 in.
   2000.200

4. Saul Baizerman
   American, born in Russia,
   1889–1957
   Aurora, 1950–57
   Hammered copper
   78 x 35 x 20 in.
   2000.201

5. Leonard Baskin
   American, 1922–2000
   Ruth and Naomi, 1979
   Bronze
   52 x 30 x 14 in.
   1998.129

6. Fernando Botero
   Colombian, born 1932
   Mother and Child, 1988
   Bronze
   81 x 45 x 27 in.
   2003.157

7. Antoine Bourdelle
   French, 1861–1929
   Hercules the Archer, 1909;
   cast 1947
   Bronze
   98 x 94 ¾ x 49 ½ in.
   Museum purchase,
   1949.17

8. Louise Bourgeois
   American, born in France,
   1911–2010
   Spider, 1996
   Bronze
   127 x 296 x 278 in.
   1998.112

9. Fritz Bultman
   American, 1919–85
   Barrier (Big Bird), 1967–70
   Bronze
   66 x 96 x 30 in.
   Gift of the artist's family,
   2003.86

10. Scott Burton
    American, 1885–1966
    Pair of Right Angle Chairs,
    1983
    Granite
    38 x 20 x 27 in.
    1998.130.1-3

11. Scott Burton
    American, 1885–1966
    Settee, 1983
    Granite
    34 x 57 x 36 ½ in.
    1998.130.1-3

12. Deborah Butterfield
American, born 1949
Restrained, 1999
Bronze
86 x 99 x 46 in.
2000.202

13. Saint Clair Cemin
American, born in Brazil,
1951
Acme, 1990
Copper
54 x 44 x 44 in.
2000.203

14. Lynn Chadwick
British, 1914–2003
Sitting Figures (2),
1979–80
Bronze
66 x 33 x 56 in.
1998.131

15. Sandro Chia
Italian, born 1946
Figure with Tear and Arrow,
1982
Bronze
72 x 38 x 53 in.
2000.204

16. Pietro Consagra
Italian, 1920–2005
*Conversation with the
Moon,* 1960
Stone and bronze
49 ½ x 50 ¼ x 4 in.
Gift of John W. Lolley,
1999.5

17. Lesley Dill
American, born 1950
*Standing Man with
Radiating Words,* 2006
Bronze
61 x 35 x 28 in.
2007.112

18. Leandro Erlich
Argentinian, born 1973
*Window and Ladder—Too
Late for Help,* 2008
Metal ladder, steel
underground structure,
fiberglass, aluminum frames
edition of 5
177 x 63 in.
Gift of Frederick Weisman
Company Fund and
De-Accession Fund,
2009.21

19. Sorel Etrog
Canadian, born in Romania,
1933
Large Pulcinella, 1965–67
Bronze
113 x 51 ½ x 27 in.
1988.132

20. Luciano Fabro
Italian, 1936–2007
*The Day Weighs on My
Night, V,* 2000
Marble with gold leaf
36 x 78 x 59 in.
2006.36

21. Audrey Flack
American, born 1931
Civitas, 1988
Patinated and gilded bronze,
glass, and marble
57 ½ x 12 x 17 in.
Gift of Susan P. and Louis K.
Meisel, 2002.305

22. Elisabeth Frink
British, 1930–93
Riace Warriors, I, II, III, IV,
1983–88
Patinated bronze
83 x 84 x 48 in.
1998.133

23. Robert Graham
American, born in Mexico,
1938–2008
Source Figure, 1991
Bronze
106 in. high overall (figure
40 in.), diameter 24 1/3 in.
2000.207

24. Barbara Hepworth
British, 1903–75
River Form, 1965
Bronze
33 ½ x 74 x 32 ½ in.
1998.134

25. Linda Howard
American, born 1934
Sunyatta, 1979
Brushed aluminum
100 x 72 x 102 in.
2000.208

26. Robert Indiana
American, born 1928
LOVE, Red Blue, 1966–97
Aluminum and acrylic
polyurethane enamel
72 x 72 x 36 in.
2004.119

27. Jean-Robert Ipoustéguy
French, 1920–2006
Grand Val de Grâce, 1977
Bronze
90 x 54 x 60 in.
1998.135

28. Menashe Kadishman
Israeli, born 1932
Open Suspense, 1968
Cor-Ten steel
120 ½ x 87 x 15 in.
1998.136

29. Anish Kapoor
British, born in India, 1954
Untitled, 1997
Stainless steel
77 ½ x 39 ¼ x 39 ¼ in.
2011.1

30. Ida Kohlmeyer
American, 1912–97
Rebus 3D-89-3, 1989
Painted aluminum
109 ½ x 97 x 36 in.
1998.137

31. Gaston Lachaise
American, born in France,
1882–1935
Heroic Man, 1928–35
Bronze
99 x 50 x 32 in.
2000.209

32. Jacques Lipchitz
American, born in Lithuania,
1891–1973
Sacrifice III, 1949–57
Bronze
55 x 40 x 25 in.
1998.138

33. Seymour Lipton
American, 1903–86
Cosmos, 1973
Nickel silver on monel
metal
70 x 73 x 36 in.
1998.139

34. René Magritte
Belgian, 1898–67
The Labors of Alexander,
1967
Cast bronze in two pieces
25 x 60 x 41 in.,
axe: 52 ¾ in.
Gift of Muriel Bultman
Francis, 1971.37

35. Aristide Maillol
French, 1861–44
Venus Without Arms, 1922
Bronze
69 ¼ in. x 19 x 14 in.
2006.35

36. Paul Manship
American, 1885–66
Tortoise, 1916; cast 1998
Bronze
25 x 49 x 26 in.
2000.210.

37. Giacomo Manzù
Italian, 1908–91
Large Seated Cardinal, 1983
Bronze
87 x 44 ¾ x 58 1/8 in.
Gift of Walda Besthoff and
the Edgar Stern Family
Fund, 2009.1

38. Allan McCollum
American, born 1944
Perfect Vehicles, 1988
MoorGlo on cast cement
78 x 36 x 36 in.
1998.140, 2010.145

39. Henry Moore
British, 1898–1986
Reclining Mother and Child,
1975
Bronze
94 ½ x 53 ½ x 47 ½ in.
1998.141

40. Jesús Moroles
American, born 1950
Las Mesas Bench, 1989
Granite
156 x 66 x 56 in.
2000.211

41. Masayuki Nagare
Japanese, born 1923
Bachi, 1979
Red granite
72 x 30 x 8 in.
1998.142

42. Minoru Niizuma
Japanese, 1930–98
Castle of the Eye, II, 1973
Marble
112 x 25 x 25 in.
1998.143

43. Isamu Noguchi
American, 1904–88
Rain Mountain, 1982
Galvanized steel
95 ½ x 24 x 21 in.
Gift of Mrs. P. Roussel
Norman, 1991.45

44. Claes Oldenburg and Coosje
van Bruggen
American, born in Sweden,
1929, and American, born in
the Netherlands, 1942–
2009
Corridor Pin, Blue, 1999
Edition 3/3
Stainless steel
255 x 256 x 16 in.
2004.118

45. Jean-Michel Othoniel
French, born 1964
Tree of Necklaces, 2002
Glass and stainless steel
70 in. (each necklace)
The River Branch
Foundation, 2002.209.1-6

46. Jaume Plensa
Catalan, born 1955
Overflow, 2005
Stainless steel
88 x 96 x 100 in.
Museum Purchase, Sydney
and Walda Besthoff Fund,
2008.133

47. Arnaldo Pomodoro
Italian, born 1926
*A Battle: For the Resistance
Fighters*, 1971
Bronze and stainless steel
149 x 141 x 141 in.
1998.144

48. Rona Pondick
American, born 1952
Monkeys, 1998–2001
Stainless steel
41 ¼ x 66 x 85 ½ in.
2003.84

49. Laila Pullinen
Finnish, born 1933
The Wader, 1996
Granite and bronze
60 x 23 ¼ x 15 ½ in.
Gift of Dr. and Mrs. Herbert
Kaufman, 2004.136

50. Pierre-Auguste Renoir
French, 1841–1919
Venus Victorious, 1914
Bronze
70 x 45 x 26 ¼ in.
2003.85

51. George Rickey
American, 1907–2002
Four Lines Oblique, 1973–77
Stainless steel
240 in. high (blades are
each 96 in. long)
1998.145

52. Auguste Rodin
French, 1840–1917
*Monumental Head of Jean
d'Aire (from The Burghers of
Calais)*, c. 1884–86; head
enlarged 1909–10
Bronze
28 ¾ x 19 7/8 x 22 ½ in.
Gift of the Iris and B. Gerald
Cantor Foundation, 2009.33

53. George Rodrigue
American, born 1944
We Stand Together, 2005
Steel, aluminum, chrome
and acrylic paint
96 x 55 x 53 ¾ in.
Gift in Memory of Mignon
McClanahan Wolfe,
2007.23

54. Richard Rosenblum
American, 1940–2000
Adam, 1990–95
Bronze
118 x 30 x 43 in.
Gift of Nancy L. Rosenblum,
2000.212

55. Alison Saar
American, born 1956
Travelin' Light, 1999
Bronze
82 x 24 x 18 in.
Gift from the family and
friends of Sunny Norman on
the occasion of her 90th
birthday, 2001.248

56. Augustus Saint-Gaudens
American, born in Ireland,
1848–1907
Diana, originally modeled
1886; cast 1985
Bronze with gilding
110 x 59 x 22 ½ in.
2010.144

57. Michael Sandle
British, born 1936
The Drummer, 1985
Bronze
106 x 38 ½ x 55 in.
1998.146

58. George Segal
American, 1924–2000
*Three Figures and Four
Benches*, 1979
Painted bronze
52 x 144 x 58 in.
1998.147

59. Joel Shapiro
American, born 1941
Untitled, 1991
Bronze
84 x 125 x 54 in.
1998.213

60. Kenneth Snelson
American, born 1927
Virlane Tower, 1981
Stainless steel
540 x 162 x 162 in.
1998.148

61. Stephen de Staebler
American, 1933–2011
*Standing Man with
Outstretched Arm*, 1987
Bronze
86 ½ x 50 ½ x 35 ½ in.
2000.205

62. Ossip Zadkine
French, born in Russia,
1890–1967
La Poetesse, 1953
Bronze
31 x 64 x 24 in.
1998.149

63. William Zorach
American, born in Lithuania,
1887–1966
Future Generations,
1942–47
Bronze
39 x 19 x 14 in.
Museum purchase in
memory of Richard Koch,
2002.183

This edition © 2011 New Orleans Museum of Art and Scala Publishers Ltd.

First published in 2011 by
Scala Publishers Ltd
Northburgh House
10 Northburgh Street
London EC1V 0AT, UK
www.scalapublishers.com

In association with
New Orleans Museum of Art
1 Collins Diboll Circle
New Orleans, Louisiana 70124
USA
www.noma.org

British Library Cataloguing-in-Publication Data:
A catalogue record for this book is available from the British Library.

ISBN: 978-1-85759-738-7

Project Manager and Copy Editor:
Stephanie Emerson
Designer: Inglis Design
Image and Copyright Assistance:
Clea Hance, Hillary Lowry, and Taylor Murrow
Produced by Scala Publications Ltd.,
New York and London

Printed and bound in China
10 9 8 7 6 5 4 3 2 1

Front Cover:
Louise Bourgeois, *Spider*, 1996 and Robert Indiana, *LOVE Red Blue*, 1966–97.
Art Louise Bourgeois Trust/Licensed by VAGA, New York City, NY

Back Cover:
Pierre-Auguste Renoir, *Venus Victorious*, 1914, and Antoine Bourdelle, *Hercules the Archer*, 1909; cast 1947

Title page:
Minoru Niizuma, *Castle of the Eye, II*, 1973